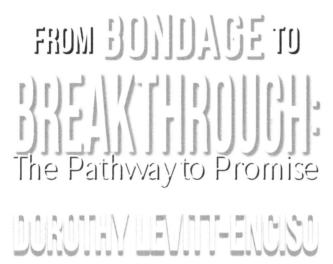

FROM BONDAGE TO BREAKTHROUGH:
The Pathway to Promise

DOROTHY LEVITT-ENCISO

Advanced Praise for *From Bondage to Breakthrough: The Pathway to Promise:*

"Some would say 'not possible' if they knew this life story's author, Dorothy, today. I have watched her for many years, press her way through adversity. She loves the Lord Jesus Christ more than many. She is Apostolic, and this story demonstrates the power of the Gospel. Through this story, many will be set free to know the true love of God. You are blessed to read these pages, and be full of thanksgiving."
~ Troy W. Shurte, Pastor, Souls Harvest, St. Cloud, Florida

"This is the story of an amazing woman who had many challenges in her life from the day she was born. Through no fault of her own, Dorothy went through one trauma after another in a very short period. People who should have loved her well as a child did not or could not. I don't think I'll ever understand why God allows such things to happen to a child, except for the undeniable fact that as He brought Dorothy out of the darkness, she was raised into His glorious light. She has become that beacon to show others the way out of their own darkness. The Bible assures us that as we are comforted by God, we will be able to comfort others. Dorothy's story, and her victories in Jesus give us all hope in the midst of things we have or are struggling with.

There is always a way out and up. I highly recommend this book for encouragement and hope in troubling times."
~ Freddi Woodford, Executive Director, Love INC (In the Name of Christ), Broward County, Florida

"I meant to take a day or two to read the Preview of Dorothy's story, but once I picked it up, I couldn't put it down until all was read. It's hard to imagine all the troubles Dorothy had to endure from such an early age. I keep thinking about my own grandchildren, knowing that I would go to the ends of the earth to keep everyone of them from having to ever suffer so. I am anxious to read the rest of the story, and learn about Dorothy's 'breakthrough.'"
~ Pam Garfinkle, the publisher's mother

"The beauty of following Jesus is built of the stories of souls who have been transformed from the depths of despair to destinations of divine placement and purpose. This book, *From Bondage to Breakthrough: The Pathway to Promise,* tracks the story of another broken beginning which the Lord remakes into something beautiful and good. Hope awaits you in these pages.'"
~ David T. Elms, Pastor, Cathedral of Pentecost, Davie, Florida

From Bondage to Breakthrough:
The Pathway to Promise

by Dorothy Levitt-Enciso

Emery Press, LLC
Fort Lauderdale, FL
www.emerypressbooks.com

First Edition – July 2022

For additional information contact Emery Press Books: wendyg@emerypressbooks.com.

Permissions: Jesus, I'll Never Forget by Barge/Odom/Rogers © 2001 Slickey Music. All rights reserved. Used by permission.

ISBN (Trade): 978-1-7364295-7-0
ISBN (eBook): 978-1-7364295-8-7

Editing & Layout Design by Wendy C. Garfinkle
Cover design by Sweet 15 Designs
Author Photo by Chelsie Enciso

To anyone who has ever been in bondage to sin, whether by chains of your own forging, or as a result of the abuse and neglect you were forced to endure.
Jesus is your Pathway to Promise.

Table of Contents

Foreword

I have known Dorothy and her daughters Brittany and Chelsie for almost 20 years. During that time, I've observed Dorothy's life, and heard various parts of the story she relates in this book, but working with her on the construction of this memoir was the first time I heard it from the beginning and in such detail. We share some commonalities: both survivors of child sex abuse, both single mothers from the time our children were small, both endured financial struggles, and the uncertainty that comes with raising child(ren) without a present father.

But here's where our paths diverge. While I was raised in a loving Christian home, Dorothy had no such spiritual foundation or strong family ties. Yet she persevered. She was tried in the fires of abandonment, abuse, neglect, and humiliation, and still, she has risen, time and again, like the proverbial phoenix from the ashes, by the grace and mercy of our Lord Jesus Christ.

When I think of the life Dorothy now lives, the strength of her faith, the love and compassion she exudes for those who have similar tales to tell, one of my favorite passages of scripture comes to mind, found in Isaiah 43:1b-3a (NKJV): "Fear not, for I have redeemed you; I have called you by your name; You are Mine. When you pass through the waters, I will be with you; And through the rivers, they shall not overflow you. When you walk through the fire, you shall not be burned, Nor shall the flame scorch you. For I am the Lord your God."

It is an honor to call Dorothy Levitt-Enciso my friend, and it's been a privilege to walk with her along the journey to telling her story and releasing it into the world, as a ministry to others who may be or have been in the midst of experiences similar to Dorothy's. I can promise you, if you connect with her, she will be happy to pray with you, be a shoulder to lean on, and offer words of encouragement and support.

Be encouraged as you read this story of one who has walked the road from Bondage to Breakthrough, and discovered the Pathway to Promise through our Lord and Savior, Jesus Christ.

Wendy C. Garfinkle, Editor/Publisher
Hollywood, Florida, July 2022

Introduction: How it Began

"YOU WILL NEVER AMOUNT TO ANYTHING!!!!"

I grew up hearing this, and believed those words for a long time.

One evening in the summer of 1969, when I was just 3 years old and my brother was 5, my life changed when my mother dropped us off at the local day care/night care center.

I remember a sinking feeling in the pit of my stomach when I asked my mom, "When are you coming back, mommy?"

Her answer was vague. "After I come back from dancing."

Despite not being able to understand what was going on, I still remember feeling that something was wrong. I tossed and turned all that night.

The next day, no mother.

She didn't come the day after that, either.

For three days, I cried and cried, wet the bed, and fought with my brother.

My mother never came back for us; never called.

Apparently, my mom told the day care workers that she was all we had left, that all of our other relatives had died.

My parents had divorced by this time, and mom had primary custody of us, so there was no way, I guess, for my dad to know that we had been left with strangers.

It wasn't until I was writing this book that I discovered the reason she left – years of physical abuse at the hands of my father.

I still don't know, though, why she didn't just take us with her when she decided to disappear, and since she died in 2002, I might never know.

But at the time, I was traumatized, and the only thing that mattered was that I wanted my mother.

I can remember one of the child care workers saying that she was calling someone, and the next thing I knew, police officers were there, asking me all kinds of questions. What was my mom's name? Where did I live?

How in the world was I supposed to know that? I was 3 years old! I was a complete basket case!

They kept my brother and me separate, and I never understood why they chose to separate us.

This was the beginning of a very hard life for us.

When the police couldn't locate my mother – or any other relative – I was taken to one foster home, and my brother was taken to a different foster home. I kept asking where my brother was, no one would answer me.

When I got to my first foster home, I was greeted with smiles. I walked in to the house and immediately began asking for my mama! I didn't understand, why was I there? What did I do wrong? Where was my brother?

It would be a few years before I was able to see him again.

I wasn't there for very long, maybe a week or so before someone came to pick me up.

I asked, "Can I go home now"?

The answer was, "The family that you will be staying with is very nice."

Apparently, the foster homes that I was staying in were only temporary until they could find a more permanent home.

I DIDN'T CARE IF THEY WERE NICE! I wanted MY MAMA!!! Where was she? What did they do with her? Why did I have to be there? Didn't she love us anymore?

Those questions were never answered. I was so broken! I was not able to think about anything except the fact that I could not be home with my mom and dad. What did I do that was so wrong at 3 years old?

Years later I found out that one of my aunts tried to take me and my brother out of foster care so that we could go and live with her, however my grandmother prevailed, leaving us to the tender mercies of the foster care system.

I'm not sure how many foster homes I was in from the ages of 3 to 7, but it was a lot!

My brother & I in 1968.

Chapter 1: Bondage Settling In

AGES 3 TO 7 WERE ONE BIG BLUR FOR ME. I only remember bits and pieces. Experience – and mental health professionals – says that this was probably my mind protecting me from the emotional trauma of a dramatic upheaval at such a young age.

In one of the homes, I remember listening to one of the other children cursing, and then all of a sudden MY head was being flushed down a commode.

"Dorothy, this is what happens to people who have filthy mouths."

This was one of the times I was blameless, but despite my protestations of innocence, the parents would not listen to me.

At some point between those years, my father must have found us, because at 7 years old, I was removed from the current foster home and sent to live with my dad, who, at the time, was living in his mother's (granny's) house.

My brother and I had been reunited, and we were now living at my grandmother's house with several of her adult children, and their husbands and their children.

My grandmother told me that my mom told HRS that my family was dead! Which I found odd, because my grandmother had 8 children! The HRS just took my mom's word as truth? My grandmother also said that they looked everywhere for me and my brother! Really? I wondered about that, I mean, how hard did she *really* look?

It should maybe not be such a surprise that HRS (properly, the Florida Department of Health and Rehabilitative Services) either wasn't able to find any family for my brother and I, or did not do more than a cursory search for family, because, as the largest social services agency in the state at that time, HRS – unaffectionally dubbed in some circles as "Home (W)Recking Service," was also the most problem-plagued agency in the state of Florida. So much so that in 1996, then-Governor Lawton Chiles signed legislation dividing this monstrosity into two smaller agencies – the Department of Health, and the Department of Children and Family Services.

But of course, in 1974, that change was more than two decades – and many, many foster homes – in my future.

At the age of 7, I didn't know how to bathe properly, comb my hair, or any of the normal hygienic things that a young girl should know how to do. None of my foster parents ever took the time to show me good hygiene, and none of the other fosters cared to do so, either.

I felt like we were only at my grandmother's house because we were my dad's children. On good days, when granny was in a good mood, or if she didn't have anywhere to go, we children were allowed to play in the house. On other days, she made us sit in a chair and read the Bible out loud.

This is when the abuse began.

Granny's husband was the same age as my father. My step-grandfather was a predator who would come into my room at night and sexually assault me.

As soon as I heard the door knob turning, I would hold myself very still and small, the covers wrapped tight around me, and pretend to be asleep. But he would always wake me up, and the covers were small defense against him. His skin was always drenched in the stink of cigarettes, and bile coated my throat every time he was near.

When I tried to tell my grandmother, she accused me of lying, and so the abuse continued.

One day when we were outside playing, granny was gone somewhere, and my step-grandfather stayed to watch the kids. As usual, he forced us kids outside and locked the door behind us.

I was thirsty and had to use the bathroom, so I peeked in the backdoor window to see him doing to my 4 year old cousin the same thing he did to me every night.

Anger and terror filled me in equal measure. I banged on the door and yelled as loud as I could for him to stop! I did not stop until he did!

Thank goodness he did not retaliate against me. I think he knew if he did, I would make sure everyone heard what he did to me.

Years later I found out that several other of my girl cousins who lived there also fell prey to his abuse.

My dad never knew what was occurring in that house until I was much older, after I had my children.

Dad came over to spend some time with the girls that particular day, and we began talking about my childhood. I was trying to piece together my past, and was telling him things I remembered, which included things my step-grandfather did to me.

I never knew my dad's face could get so red so fast; he was boiling mad!

Suddenly, he could not bear to hear anymore. He got up, said goodbye to me and the girls, and left.

We've never spoken of it since, because I didn't ever want to see him that angry again.

We kids spent most of our days outside until dark. We were not allowed in the house at all unless we had to use the bathroom or needed a drink of water. If we were thirsty, we had to knock on the locked door, and ask: "May I please have a drink of water?"

We were handed a really large cup of water that we had to drink while standing on the porch, until the very last drop.

Needless to say, we did not knock on the door that often; the water hose became our thirst-quencher.

In school, at 8 years old, I was the punching bag for several bullies. They also called me names and told me how bad I smelled, which wasn't anything I didn't already know, but it was still humiliating to be under the spotlight for such a negative reason.

On several occasions I had to wear my dad's size 10 shoes to school because I did not have my own shoes, and, of course, the bullies were even more entertained.

One day I just couldn't take anymore. I followed one of the girls home after school without her knowing. I marked her house in my mind, went home, put all my things away, and came back to her house. I knocked on the door, and when her mom answered, I asked if she could come out to play. Her mom said sure, and went to get her daughter.

When the girl came to the door, I reached up and grabbed one of her dangling Santa Claus earrings, pretending to admire it. When I had a good hold on it, I yanked that earring right out of her ear, and took off running!

Somehow I never got in trouble for that, and the kids at that school never bullied me again.

I think this is where I developed the mentality that I would take, and take, and take some more until I had enough, and then when I had enough, EVERYONE found out about it.

I still struggle with this sometimes, but mostly, I have learned how to give these things to God to handle, since He does a much better job. I have also learned that when you really pray for those who hurt you, God blesses your life even more.

While living at my grandmother's house, we went to church with her every Sunday. She was a member of a Nazarene church. I liked going to Sunday school, because the people were really nice, and I was able to do arts and crafts.

I remember many times after Sunday school, we would all go back into the Sanctuary, and I just couldn't wait for the altar call to come. My heart hurt! I was trying in my own way to deal with these things that I went through. I would go and kneel at the altar where there was always a picture of Jesus on the wall. I would look into His eyes, and seek for His help. My tears were real! I really needed help!

Everyone else I turned to turned their back on me or just didn't listen, but somehow, I always felt such a release telling God about it. Even those things that happened in the still of the night.

Though I was smart in spite of the many moves between homes and schools during my formative years, I was not able to show it on paper.

One particular school decided to test me, to see where I was academically. I was in the 3rd grade, but reading on a college level. They tried to place me in the gifted class, but socially, I was not blending in too well. I skipped school often, so it's a wonder I graduated with my age group.

I skimped money where ever I could find it. I would walk around the neighborhood with my little red wagon collecting glass bottles and soda cans, because back then you could get $.05 to $.10 per bottle or can, and then I would take them to the closest 7-11 store to collect my money.

With the money I received from the bottles and cans, I would buy little snacks to supplement my daily meals, which consisted only of supper at night. Those dinners were small, due to the fact that my grandmother was very poor.

Most times, I could not stand the food, so I would throw it under the table to the dog. I got caught one night, though, when I threw sauerkraut under the table and even the dog wouldn't eat it!

This was before the days of the National School Lunch Program that provides daily low-cost or free lunches to school children each day, so without the money I made collecting cans and bottles, I might have had an even harder time learning in school, from hunger.

My brother was involved in a little league baseball team, and learned to play the guitar. Being in foster homes did not seem to have bothered him much in the early years. He always seemed to have it all together when we were kids, and was definitely the favorite of the two of us.

I was the troubled child.

Back then, my brother didn't want anything to do with me. He did not allow me to play with him, or be around him when he was with his friends.

After a while, my aunts and uncles took their children and moved out, leaving my brother and me as the only children in the house.

I was so lonely that when I was in the back yard playing and singing, I would pretend that I had a line of all the teachers I liked standing up against the wall, and I would put on a concert for them. (Maybe that's why my brother did not want anything to do with me.)

Singing seemed to dull the pain! When I was punished, or confined to my room, I would stand on a chair, and, using my hair brush as a microphone, sing at the top of my lungs to drown out the pain.

God, please make it all stop! I often asked God what I did that was so wrong to deserve all of this.

I never got my answer.

As I grew older, I realized that I didn't do anything to deserve all those struggles; sin, and man's free will, were to blame.

Dad, holding framed photos of my brother & me.

Me, with Chelsie & Aaliyah, Mother's Day, 2021.

Chapter 2: The Struggle

BEFORE AN OFF-THE-TRACK ACCIDENT that left him incapacitated, and after he left the Air Force, my dad, John "Jack" Levitt, was a professional stock car driver. Since he was also a mechanic and a welder, he was able, with help from a friend, to build his race car from the wheels up. There were many days when he was home working on that car, my brother and I were outside with him, either cleaning his tools, or fetching them for him.

My dad, Airman Basic John Sidney Levitt, in 1962.

I don't know how many races he won, but I was so proud that he was my daddy!

On several occasions we were able to go the race track in Hialeah, Daytona, or Indianapolis to watch him race. He would rent a big king cab truck, tow his stock car on the back, and my brother and I rode in the bed of the truck the whole way, with plenty of blankets to keep us warm. I would make signs that said "Go Big Red!" (his racing nickname, because of his red hair) to hold up in the stands for him.

He did win a few times, and we were able to crawl into his stock car with him when he took his victory lap.

There were also times when we sat in the bleachers watching him race, we would see him hit a wall, or spin out, or watch his car catch on fire. I would be anxious, those times, until I saw him emerge from his car, maybe a little shaken and worse for the wear, but I always breathed easier then.

On the way home, we would stop at an IHOP to eat, which was always a treat.

I don't remember much about these times, because they were so few and far between, but I will never forget them, as long as I live. Because when he was gone, my brother and I suffered much physical and sexual abuse. It wasn't often that my brother fell victim to this, but nevertheless, we both were victimized.

At about 2:00 one morning in 1974, when we were still living in Fort Lauderdale at my grandmother's, a sudden knock on my bedroom window terrified me awake out of a sound sleep.

I looked out the window to see a police officer shining his flashlight in my face.

I opened the window. "Can I help you?" I asked him, hesitantly.

"I'm sorry to disturb you, young lady," he said. "I tried to knock on the front door, but I guess no one heard me."

"Okay," I said.

"Are you John Levitt's daughter?"

"Yes." I felt myself pale. "Did something happen to my daddy?"

"Well, he was in an accident..."

I jumped up out of bed, ran to my granny's room, and banged on her door till she opened it. "There's a policeman at the door! Something bad happened to daddy!"

We all dressed in a hurry, piled into the car, and headed to the hospital.

Apparently, after working a full day, my dad took his then-girlfriend, Roseanne, out on a date, and then drove her home. After he dropped her off, he fell asleep at the wheel, and ended up hitting a light pole head on, knocking his head on the bar between the windshield and his driver's side window. He crushed his skull so severely that the doctors gave him only a 30 percent chance to live; in fact, they didn't expect him to make it through the night.

I was only 8 years old, so they would not allow me to go in to see him. We spent the night in the lobby at the hospital. I never prayed so hard in all my life! I needed my daddy! I did not know God, but because I went to my grandmother's Nazarene church, I knew *of* God.

Miraculously, my dad made it through the night!

This was so hard for me to grasp. I was finally able to live with my dad again, and then this happened!

One day, after making an "A" on my homework at school, I went to visit my dad to show him the good grade. I wanted to make him proud, and just knew that seeing my "A" would make him feel better.

One of the nurses saw how much I wanted to go and see him, so she snuck me in. But I wasn't ready for what I was about to see.

My dad's face drooped on the left side from where they had to take out the part of his skull that was crushed in the accident. For some reason, they didn't put a plate in his head so that he would look normal. He had a scar running down the whole left side of his face from where they put in the wire mesh that was holding up his left eye.

My dad, years after his accident.

This was my first time seeing my daddy after his accident, and no one prepared me, but somehow, I was able to look past all of that and see that he was just my daddy.

When I showed him my picture, all he could do was smile. But that was reward enough for me!

The road to recovery was a long one for him. He had to learn how to walk, read, and write all over again. When he got out of the hospital, he just was not the same. We had to be careful not to upset him because he would have a seizure.

Roseanne, the girlfriend he had taken home after their date prior to having the accident that changed his life – and ours – convinced him to get married, even though he didn't really know what was going on.

His now-wife and her two children, Katherine and Jimmy, took complete advantage of his condition, and walked all over him. Katherine was around my age, and Jimmy was younger than me.

Roseanne convinced dad to move out of granny's house, which should have been a positive change, since it meant I would be beyond the reach of my granny's husband. But though the sexual abuse stopped, the physical and emotional abuse continued.

My new stepmother would lock me in my room for days at a time, denying me food and drink. I managed to figure out how to get my door open, and I would sneak out at night, steal bread from the freezer, and drink the cat's water.

While maturity tells me that my stepmother probably wasn't as terrifying as 8-year-old me thought she was, back then, her long, bushy black hair and large, bucked teeth appeared "wicked-looking" to me, to the extent that I had actual nightmares about her. I would be so scared that I would crawl under the bed, and spend the night hiding from her. Other nights, while lying in my bed, I would see a figure coming through the window with a knife raised towards me. Many nights, I cried myself to sleep for fear of her.

One particular, rainy night she was so upset at me for something, that she opened the back door, and forced me outside into the rain. The thunder and lightning frightened me.

I don't know if it was because I was so young, or if it was because she terrified me, but I could have sworn that I saw Satan himself out there in that rain! I heard him speak, and tell me that I would never make it to heaven, which made me cry more!

I screamed, "YES, I WILL!"

That day, I developed a fight to live. I was going to disprove those words that echoed in my head every day.

I started screaming on the top of my lungs for my dad's wife to let me back in the house. I didn't stop screaming until she finally did.

It wasn't enough for Roseanne to terrorize me herself, she would also instruct her daughter to beat up on me while Roseanne held down my arms and her son held my legs, preventing me from fighting back.

Once, I ran away. The police picked me up and took me to the police station where I tried to tell them what was going on. All they did was call my dad and stepmother to pick me up.

So then I tried something different. After school, I would go to the backyard, climb the tree, and just sit up there until it was too dark for me to stay outside, and then I went in.

This was my secret place. Nothing mattered when I was up there. I could just relax, and not be bothered by anyone.

I tried to run away again when I was 10. I hid in neighbors' backyards for a few hours, and then I walked until I could not walk anymore.

I would always get caught by the police, though, and brought right back home. I tried to explain to the officers what was going on, but they wouldn't listen to me.

One day I hid in the back of my dad's car. It felt so good to have some peace and quiet, and I stayed there for hours. It didn't last long enough, though, because daddy got in the car to go look for me, and I was busted. After I got yelled at, I was able to go to bed.

The discipline my dad learned in the Air Force carried over into his parenting, so everything had to be spotless, or else. One particular day, my brother and I were washing the dishes. I tried for hours to get the burnt blackness off of the bottom of a pan, and I failed. So when daddy came to check, he started yelling at me for taking so long with little to show for my effort.

I yelled back that I tried to get the pan clean, but I couldn't.

That was the first time I felt the wrath of my dad's fist.

One chipped tooth and broken heart later, I learned not to upset my dad.

Eventually, Roseanne put me in a facility for troubled kids. This is where I received my first kiss from a boy – in a tunnel on the playground.

By that time, my academic level had fallen to the 2nd grade, even though I was 11 years old and supposed to be in the 5th grade. I weighed only 88 lbs., from the constant malnutrition.

My brother was still the favorite. He knew how to play it cool, so they kept him at home. He never stood up for me to our stepmother, and I never understood that.

I liked it there, in the facility for troubled kids; I was making friends, and there was structure. They taught me how to take care of myself, and I was starting to come out of my shell a little bit.

The facility got me a little clock radio that I would listen to at night, and every song I heard, I associated to my life.

The words "Baby, don't leave me," I associated to "Daddy, don't leave me." Et cetera.

Music was my coping mechanism.

I was only in that facility for 8 months when my daddy and Roseanne came to pick me up, telling me that we were moving to Vidor, Texas.

We were three days on the road, and I was excited to be with my brother and my dad again.

We found a home and moved in, but just as quick as we moved in, *she* started again. My brother and I became the enemy. We were the ones keeping her from having complete control over our daddy.

She never said those words exactly, of course, but we knew. She was the one in control; daddy could barely speak, much less make a decision.

We were in Texas for 1 month, and then, four days before Christmas, she decided to put me in another facility for troubled kids. And this time, she sent my brother there with me. Daddy was not able to stand up for himself, much less for us, so he just left us in there.

Once again, we were traumatized, betrayed, and rejected.

But I was not alone this time. My brother was on the second floor with the boys, and I was on the first floor with the girls, and we were together at meal times.

This is where I learned how to dominate and manipulate in the card game of Spades. I also became a very good pool shark.

My brother, on the other hand, began to display anger issues. Many times the caretakers would give him a shot of

Thorazine and put him in a padded room to calm him down

After a while, it became home, and we adapted and integrated. I learned how to crochet and spin wool, and a bunch of other neat things while I was there.

The facility put on a huge talent show every year that drew more than 2,000 people, and I decided to join in.

I was a nervous wreck, and didn't know if I could pull off the songs I chose to sing, but somehow I managed to do it, and received a standing ovation. Maybe it was because they felt sorry for me, but either way, it felt really good.

This is where I was told that I had a good voice, and that I should use it more often. I'm not sure how true that was back then, but it certainly did help me through a lot of things in my life.

This was also where I started really smoking. I had smoked before on the sly. I don't remember where I obtained the cigarettes, but they were menthol. No one ever caught me; I think the staff knew, they just never said anything to me.

The staff kept asking me, "Why are you here? You don't belong here."

They must have called my dad to tell him that, because it wasn't too long after that he came with Roseanne to inform me that he no longer wanted me. He wanted my brother, but he thought I should go back into foster care.

It was probably his wife's idea, but I was devastated … rejected all over again. So I lost track of my brother and my dad for a third time.

Why was I not allowed to have a nice loving family? My grandmother had 8 children, where were they all? Why did they not step in to help us? I was told that they were too busy spending my inheritance that my biological grandfather left me before he died. He left us each an acre in Ocala, Florida, and a lump sum of money that would have carried me a long way. But since my grandfather died before I was born, I don't know how true all of that actually was.

With the previous foster homes, the abuse at the hands of my step-grandfather, and Roseanne, I don't know how I was still mentally stable. Maybe I wasn't really stable at all; in fact, I was labeled emotionally disturbed, and was more than Roseanne could handle.

Who knows?

Sad to say, I was able to deal with the rejection better this time. Yes, I missed my dad, but deep inside, I knew it was Roseanne, and not my dad who made this decision, so that helped me to deal with things a little better.

Two months later, I was 12, and a family in Tyler, Texas, said they wanted me. They had 8 children of their own, but decided to take another one.

They were really nice to me. We went water skiing at their lake house, swimming, and other fun activities.

I started to excel in school. In Hogg Middle School, as well as at Robert E. Lee High School, I ran track, and cross-country. I played girls' basketball, and varsity volleyball. I won lots of ribbons and trophies, but lost them over the years because of the frequent moves.

I had found something that I was good at besides music, and it made me feel free. It was my outlet.

This family was a part of a program that raised funds to help children like me in foster care have a better life. On a few of those fund raisers, they had a JR Rodeo. I was able to race my horse in the barrel races. I did not win, but it sure was a lot of fun!

My foster parents tried to pursue adoption, and this is when I found out my mom was still alive. She wanted nothing to do with me. Another rejection. But my dad refused to relinquish his rights as my father. He still wanted to be my dad, even though he was not capable of taking care of me. So, I remained with that family for two years as a long-term foster.

I must have still had issues they couldn't deal with, because I had to move again. To this day, I don't know what I did to make them get rid of me. I did have a mouth, so maybe they decided that they did not want to deal with that anymore.

For the next few years, it was back to temporary foster homes for me. I'd spend a week here, a month there. I was so sick and tired of moving! I just could not take it anymore, and told my case worker that I was tired of moving.

My next foster home was in Conroe, Texas. I was now 14 years old, and had started to act out a bit under the guise of joking.

One night, after a girl who had been bullying me fell asleep, I decided to teach her a lesson. I got some tooth paste, and shampoo, and very carefully poured it all over her face and hair. I was careful not to wake her, and yes, she slept through the whole thing. Then I got a bowl of warm water and stuck her hand in it, because someone once told me that this would make her go to the bathroom on herself, and I thought this would be hilarious! I could picture it in my mind so vividly that I would laugh at the very thought of her waking up like that.

The next morning, when she woke up, the whole home heard her! I knew I wouldn't be there long after that.

The house parents questioned me.

"Yes," I declared, "I did it. She's always bullying me, and I wanted to get back at her."

But this was considered a "violent" act, so I had to go. I was kind of glad to go, because I'm sure she would have tried to beat me to death in retaliation.

So my case worker came back to get me. I was able to share a lot of how I felt with her. She seemed to be the only one who actually cared enough to listen. I could tell her anything, and she made sure that she set me straight when I needed it as well.

She decided once we were down the road a piece that she was just too tired to drive; she was swerving all over the road, to the point that I called attention to it. I had taken Driver's Ed classes in high school, and had my permit, so I offered to drive. Imagine my surprise when she allowed me to drive from Conroe to Waco so she could get some sleep!

I must have been a good driver because she went right to sleep and didn't wake up until we arrived.

My next move was to the Methodist Children's Home in Waco. This was a group home setting, a huge property with many mansion-like homes, each containing several rooms. The boys lived on one side of the property, and the girls on the other side.

This is where I met my first best friend, Debbie Parks. She was beautiful, and had the most infectious smile, yet she was so down-to-earth. I loved being around her. We became instant friends and were inseparable. We sang in the choir, played basketball, and got into trouble together.

It felt good to be able to sing again! This was the best therapy for me. They tried to put me into regular therapy sessions, but I did all of the talking. No one ever had any advice for helping me deal with all of the emotion baggage I had acquired throughout my life, so I had to figure things out for myself.

OLDER GIRLS' TEAM members are (l-r first row) Sandra, Dorothy, Rosa and Debbie, (l-r second row) Rosemary, Amanda, Tundra, Lisa and Ginger and Terry (in front).

Methodist Children's Home Girls Basketball Team, May 1982 – I am in the first row, 2nd from the left. My best friend at the time, Debbie Parks, is at the end of the first row.

Somehow, I pushed everything that I had previously gone through out of my head, just to deal with the current circumstances.

Looking back now, I see how God was right there the whole time. He made sure that I was okay. I'm sure I frustrated God, because I kept doing my own thing. In my defense, I really didn't know any better, but God kept me, and He never let me go.

In hind sight, I can see that He was carrying me most of the time. I NEVER did without anything, and was always well-taken care of financially.

One day, when my group of girls was coming back to our residence, it was raining hard, so we all ran up the steps onto the painted concrete porch, trying to be the first at the door. I was a good runner back then, so I was first.

When I put my hand on the window to the left of the front door to stop myself, the whole widow broke, and my arm went right through it.

I was in such shock over breaking the window. I was afraid I was going to get into trouble, and kept saying that I would find a way to pay for it, when someone said to me, "Dorothy, you're bleeding!"

The Walter William Fondren Home on the Waco Campus was where I lived whilst at the Methodist Children's Home, and it was the glass window to the left of the door (when exiting) that I stuck my arm through.

At first I just shrugged it off, because I didn't feel any pain anywhere, and then I looked down to find a huge gash in my shoulder. A big chuck of flesh was missing! At that point I started screaming and panicking! I forgot all about the window, and my promise to pay for it.

I was rushed to the hospital to where I received 11 stitches.

I did not have to pay for anything, of course, thank God!

Another time, I was swimming at the pool with all of my friends, and decided that I wanted to dive off the diving board. I was pretty good at it, but that day, for some reason, I got spooked as soon my feet left the board, and I went off to the side of the pool just in front of the side ladder.

I was relieved that my face missed it, but then my foot began to throb. I looked down, and realized that my big toe got caught under the step of the ladder. There was blood everywhere!

Again, I was taken to the hospital, where I again received 11 stitches.

Waco High School, 1982

I must have been accident prone, because not long after that I decided to dive into the shallow end of the pool. I hit the bottom face first, which resulted in breaking off one of my front teeth.

Once again, I was rushed to a doctor, who sent me to a dentist to cap my missing tooth.

In spite of all my misadventures, the Methodist Children's Home in Waco really did become home. I had lots of friends, and I felt free of family drama. But I couldn't seem to avoid self-sabotage.

One day, while I was doing my chores, one of the new girls decided to stand right in the middle of the floor I was mopping.

"Move," I ordered.

She continued to stand there, as if her feet were rooted to the floor, and just stared at me.

Beginning to grow angry, I repeated my demand, "MOVE, or I will move you!"

She didn't appear to fear my wrath. Of course, I was still rather scrawny then, so maybe it's not surprising that she didn't take me seriously. But I was about to show her my scrappy side.

I snarled, "NOW YOU WILL MOVE!" and without considering the consequences, I picked up the mop handle and swung it at her.

And I didn't miss.

Down she went. Head over heels, she tumbled down the stairs.

Turns out that she got a concussion from the fall.

The Methodist Children's Home had a zero tolerance policy for violence, and with that one incident, I crossed the line. So once again, I was relocated, this time from a home I had grown to love.

And I lost contact with Debbie, my best friend, for many years, until 2018, when she located me on Facebook.

Social media has its uses.

My next residence was a girls' wilderness camp in Groveton, Texas, for troubled girls.

I lived with a few other girls in an a-frame structure that we built from the trees that we cut down ourselves. We learned how to measure like architects, and while the plans had to be approved by a certified architect, we did all of the actual work. We cut out notches to piece the two trees together. Next, we drilled a hole, and hammered in dowel pins as wooden nails. For the roof, we cut several smaller trees, climbed up to the top of the structure, and used binder's twine to tie the trees together. Finally, we stretched a tarp over the wooden roof, and tied it down to the beams.

Though it wasn't a fully enclosed cabin, I loved every minute of building that wooden house.

At night, we eliminated into a small pot that was placed in the middle of the floor for that purpose. During the day, our latrine was a 6-foot-deep ditch that we dug ourselves. Each day, we cleaned the nighttime pot, and each day we coated the ditch with lime to keep away the smell and disease.

Our seats were fat trees that we cut down using a crosscut saw. We would have group sessions called circle-up time – anytime one of us girls had a problem with another girl, or family trouble, or some such – during which everyone, including counselors, would drop everything to sit in, listen, and offer help. Everyone was allowed to contribute advice based on our own life experiences.

One day, I was on the receiving end of one of these sessions.

I received a letter from my dad telling me that he no longer wanted anything to do with me.

Apparently, even though he and Roseanne eventually parted ways, he took up with another lady who was just as bad, and she, also, took advantage of his weakened mental state to further reject me.

Tears streamed down my face as I read the letter over and over again.

The counselors asked if I wanted to talk about it, and they all sat in silence as I talked and raged.

How could he do this to me yet again?

I loved my dad no matter what, and I knew that he wasn't able to make these kinds of decisions on his own, but that didn't mean the constant rejection hurt any less.

During the week, we would cook our meals over an open fire for breakfast, lunch, and dinner. This is how I learned to cook. For Thanksgiving, we would prepare the turkey, wrap it in foil, and bury it in a hole we dug in the ground. Then we piled hot coals on top of the bird and cooked it. That turned out to be the best-tasting turkey I had ever had. On the weekend, we were allowed to go into the chow hall for our meals.

Learning how to survive in the wilderness was an adventure I thoroughly enjoyed.

While I was learning wilderness skills, I also excelled in academics, especially in math. I was able to move ahead in my education to the point that I skipped the 10th grade entirely.

One year, we were training for the Special Olympics that was held for those with emotional and mental issues. When we got up one particular morning during training, it was 17 degrees outside. I had slept in my long johns, so on top of those, I threw on a pair of Wrangler jeans, two pairs of socks and some leg warmers, as well as a sweatshirt and a flannel shirt, and then my goose down jacket to hold in all the warmth my body had amassed during the night.

However, what I did not realize, is that the warmth began dissipating as soon as I got out of bed. So all of those layers were holding in the cold, and my body was not able to warm up.

I was training for the mile race, and as I practiced my timing, I started to feel faint, and ended up passing out on the track. The counselors carried me into the chuck hall, laid me down on one of the tables, and started CPR. When I finally revived, the counselors told me that I had gotten hypothermia, and that the next stage was blue lips!

When I questioned them, they seemed really afraid that I was going to die. My lips started turning blue, they said… But GOD!

I was coddled for the next few hours until I was well enough to get back on my feet.

They did call my dad at that point, and he rushed to the camp to assure himself that I would survive. That was the first time I had seen him in 4 years, so I was happy to see him, even under the circumstances.

I stayed at the wilderness camp for several more months, until I was allowed to visit my dad on the weekends. Due to my dad's condition, he wasn't able to care for me, so I wasn't allowed to live with him.

It was time for me to leave the girls wilderness camp, but before I left, they had a talent show, and of course, I performed.

I sang "The Rose" by Bette Midler, which had become my personal theme song, as it seemed to fit my life so well.

There was not a dry eye in the audience, because so many of them knew what I had been through.

I have always sung songs that have somehow applied to my life in one way or another.

I started 11th grade at West Orange-Stark High School, in West Orange, Texas.

The new foster parents in Orange, Texas, were really nice to me, but it was only a temporary home, and though they tried to get me to love and accept them, I had been through too much, didn't feel it was worth the effort and emotion, so while I was as respectful as I could be, I refused to get attached.

For my 15th birthday, the foster mom, who was Italian, cooked me a really nice steak dinner.

I sat down with a delighted grin to enjoy this awesome plate of food and took my first bite.

I tried to keep chewing and not react to the awful flavor that filled my mouth. But that didn't last long before I spit the bite onto my plate, and shuddered in disgust.

She gave me a hurt and startled look before hurrying to her bedroom in tears. She avoided me for a few days.

I felt bad about my reaction, but I've never been one to sugar-coat anything.

It turns out, she marinated the steaks heavily in cooking sherry. I had never tasted alcohol before then, and though cooking is supposed to make the alcohol evaporate – and maybe it did – I could not stand the taste.

Needless to say, I was not there for much longer.

I asked my case worker to keep me in the same high school, so she found another home for me to stay at in the area.

This new family seemed like my kind of people. They had a teenaged son who was a smart aleck, just like me, and a daughter who I immediately connected with. I seemed to be able to get along with the whole family, which was nice, as they would be my last foster family.

When I was a senior in West Orange-Stark High School, I met Ramona. She lived across the street, and we went to school together. Though she was 2 years younger than me, her maturity level was high for her age, so we became instant friends.

Ramona was Apostolic. At first, I couldn't understand why I had to always go over to her house, instead of her coming to mine sometimes, but it didn't matter too much, as long as we could be friends. She never failed to invite me to go to church with her, but the family I lived with went to a Salvation Army church, so I could not go with her.

I later learned that my foster family were backslidden Apostolic, which was as good an explanation as any why they would never allow me to go to church with Ramona.

I had my first real boyfriend during this time: Glen. Glen and I did a lot together. We went fishing in the river – well, craw fishing on his boat – and of course we went out to eat quite a bit. I also cooked my famous biscuits and a few other things for him.

We dated for almost two years, at which point he asked me to marry him.

I said no. I'm not really sure why, but something inside told me that I wasn't ready for marriage. I didn't really understand what it meant to have someone care for me like that.

It wasn't long after that he stopped calling me, stopped dropping by to visit me. I felt like I needed more time, but he never gave me that time; just abruptly would not return my calls.

I did really well in school. Since I had skipped the 10th grade, I only needed 1 more credit to graduate. So in my senior year, I took all electives except for English, which was the one credit I needed.

By this time, my anger had subsided somewhat, and I was becoming a preppy/country girl, but I was also the class clown.

I found that humor had become yet another of my outlets to dealing with life's troubles.

My English teacher wore polyester suits, had a nasal voice, and none of the students really liked her. On the last day of school, she proctored our final English test. I finished early, and had become a little bored waiting for the other students to finish so we could be released. The teacher left the classroom for a few minutes, and I got this wild idea to put tacks in her seat. I asked the class if they dared me to do it.

Dumb question, right? Of course they did! And I took that dare.

I ran up to her seat, rummaged through her desk, and grabbed a few tacks. I carefully placed them in her chair, pointed side up, and then ran back to my seat just before she walked back in the class.

I put my head down because I was anticipating her reaction once she sat down. Without looking down, she sat, and came right back up with a squeal. I was almost bursting with the attempt to hold in my laughter, and had to leave the room.

Thank goodness the bell rang in time for me to escape before my laughter gave me away.

I don't know if she ever found out that I was the one who put those tacks on her chair.

I saw my English teacher two weeks after graduation, and couldn't look at her without laughing!

I am not proud of this now, because I realize that I could have really hurt her.

Amazingly enough, in spite of all the challenges I faced getting there, I graduated with a 3.5 GPA, which put me in the top 10 percent of my graduating class of 319 students.

I give all the credit to God.

My senior year, the foster parents told me that if I wanted a car, I would have to earn it. I agreed. They purchased a car, and I got a job so that I could repay them.

Finally, I turned 18, and there was a family meeting in the living room. I thought for sure this was going to be a pep talk on me becoming an adult.

However, what came out of the dad's mouth was, "Tomorrow, you are to move out. I don't care where you go, but you are no longer welcome here."

Talk about getting the very air knocked out of me! But by that night, I found a live-in nanny job.

I didn't stay at that job long, however; only about a month. The father came home one night drunk and started making advances towards me. Because of my history with this type of abuse, I decided to move out that night.

I didn't know anything about having a checking account, or paying rent, electric, water, or anything else like that. I had never handled money before. But once again, God!

Ever since making friends with Ramona, I kept her in the know, whatever was going on in my life. I called her, and she told me to come to her house. The next day, her parents told me that I was welcome to stay, as long as I went to church with them. So, I did.

I went with Ramona's family to their church in Starks, Louisiana, and also to several Richard Heard revivals.

One Sunday night, while driving home from one of those revival services, we were caught in a very bad thunderstorm. Ramona and I were scared, so we decided to sing all the way home. And God helped us arrive home safely.

The next day we found out that we had been in the direct path of a tornado that had destroyed all of the homes in its wake.

My first thought was, *I don't have the Holy Ghost yet, I'm not ready to die...God protected me*!

So the next time I went to church, I made up my mind that I was going to get this Holy Ghost that everyone was talking about!

That Thursday, midweek service, I was determined to get the Holy Ghost. During the entire worship service, God dealt with me. I was sitting about 6 rows back from the front, and holding on to the back of that seat like my life depended on it.

I started crying, thinking about my life, and how I was protected from this huge tornado. I felt such a strong pull towards the altar. But it was a huge church! I was not going up there!

All of a sudden, while they were still singing, the Holy Ghost got ahold of me, and I couldn't hold back anymore. I took off running.

If you know anything about the First Pentecostal Church of Starks, you know it's HUGE! But that was nothing for me after 6 years of running track and cross-country.

I stopped at the altar, and every lady in that church immediately formed a circle around me until I prayed through. God met me there that night!

So many thoughts filled my head. *How could God love me?* Everyone else had rejected me.

Then, someone whispered in my ear, "Picture God reaching His hand down to you. He is waiting for you to reach your hand up to His."

When I finally surrendered to Him, He filled me with His precious Holy Ghost. Two weeks later, I was baptized in Jesus' Name! I don't know why I had to wait two weeks to be baptized, and I didn't know why I needed to be baptized; I didn't understand anything, but out of obedience, I did it. Just in case there was another tornado coming.

That was the most incredible experience ever! I felt God wrap His arms around me. I was safe. Life as I had known it came to an end, and life with the Holy Ghost began. For once in my life, I knew what it felt like to have hope!

Now, it was time for the healing to begin!

Chapter 3: Healing Begins

I WAS GRATEFUL to the Hamiltons for taking me in when I needed it most, but it was time for me to move out. One day after church, when Ramona's parents dropped us off at a friend's house for lunch, I saw an old abandoned church building down the street. When Ramona and I got back to her house, I told her how thankful I was for what she and her family had done for me, but it was time for me to go.

The family was already dealing with a lot from their son, I didn't want to be an added burden. I went to church with them one last time, but told them that I wasn't going back home with them. Instead, I went to that old abandon church, which turned out to be the old Starks church building that they used for storage. I was happy to find it unlocked, and so I slept there. I found clothing items that I used for church.

My residence in the building ended abruptly two weeks later, because Sister O'Brien found out about it. I don't know who spilled the beans, but she made sure to find another family in the church – the Davenports – to take me in.

The Davenports were VERY good to me, they taught me how to pray at home, how to cook, do my own taxes, and how to take care of a home. We became quite close. I learned how to care for myself, and grew in my relationship with

God quite a bit while I lived with them. I knew this would not be a permanent thing because I was an adult now, and needed a place of my own. Brother Davenport helped me find a good job, and then a place to stay.

When I started going to church, and had not finished paying off my car yet, the parents from the last foster home decided to take the car back. So since I did not have a car anymore, my job had to be close to where I lived. What I didn't expect, was that with all of the nearby jobs that I applied for, three businesses were interested in me! So I took them all, three part-time jobs at once, and still made sure that I was able to go to church; that was my lifeline! I was a waitress at Pancho's Mexican Buffet, answered phones at Olan Mills photography, and cashiered at Market Place. Because each job was part-time and within walking distance, I had no problems showing up to work on time.

While living with the Davenports, I received a visitor, my ex-boyfriend Glen's mom. I was happy to see her, because I had so many questions. But they were to go unanswered, because one of the first things that came out of her mouth threw me for a loop. She said that Glen had gotten married and was not serving God.

I was so confused! I had never associated Glen with church at all. She filled me in on his life and the circumstances that led to him backsliding.

Hurt filled my heart. Why hadn't he ever told me about God? Why had he never shared his faith with me?

I catalogued the information, and handled the heartache like everything else that had caused me pain; I tucked it away in the back of my mind – to be dealt with at a later time – and went on with my life.

Me (the taller girl in the white dress) and Connie (Glen's sister) at my first Christmas Banquet, First Pentecostal Church of Starks, Louisiana, 1984

After the Davenports taught me how to do my taxes, pay my tithes, and bills, they felt that I was now ready to live on my own. They always took me to church, and would frequently stop by to check on me. I was so grateful to them for everything! Since they lived in Maryville, I found an apartment near my jobs, which were in Orange. I moved into a small 1-bedroom duplex, where I learned how to live on my own.

Those were the toughest years of my life, but I knew to pray and read my Bible every day, which is what helped me through so many things. I could feel God taking care of me. Every night He would show me something new in His Word.

Prayer and the Word were the staples that held me together as I tried to figure out what I was supposed to do next.

One day after church, I went to my landlady's house, (she always made sure I had something to eat), and we started talking about church. She was a devout Baptist, but she listened to what I had to say. When I was done, she agreed to come to church with me the next Thursday. I was floored! She came a couple more times, and then decided Pentecost was not for her.

Soon after, she called me over to her house, and when I got there, she told me about one of the neighbors who had been watching me and had asked my landlady whether I was Apostolic. My landlady asked if I would mind paying that neighbor a visit. I said I would.

Now mind you, I was fresh out of foster homes, and had only been in church about one month. I didn't know anything about anything, but I said, "Ok, Lord, if you will help me, I will go."

When I got to the neighbor's home, she politely invited me in, and offered me a drink. It was only water, but if you know me at all, you know why I declined, but asked why she wanted to see me. She then shared her story with me. She was a drug addict and a prostitute, and she wanted help to get out of that.

"I've been watching you, Dorothy. There's something different about you, and I want what you have."

I had this HUGE lump in my throat. *Okay, GOD,* I thought, *I don't have a clue what to say to this woman, so please HELP ME!*

The still small voice of God told me to pray with her, so I did just that, but I sure wasn't expecting what happened next.

She started speaking in tongues, right there in her living room! I was shocked, but so excited at the same time.

When we finished praying, she told me that she was backslidden.

I thought, *Wow! Look at You, God! Thank you for making it possible for me to help this hungry soul make things right with You!*

I invited her to church, and she came with me. When I told Sister O'Brien what had happened, she told Pastor O'Brien. What I did NOT expect was for him to call me to the pulpit to share what God had done. There was a lot of shouting, and dancing in response to my sharing this story.

God did it yet again! And He used little ole me! A nobody, a reject, so to speak!

I never saw this woman again. I can only pray that she is still serving God.

God started to use me in a lot of ways from that point forward. I went to nursing home ministry, I sang in the choir, and with prompting from Sister O'Brien, I even sang solos and in a trio or two.

One day as I was sitting at my kitchen table, I decided to call the Texas Department of Family and Protective Services to find out if I could get a copy of my records. At that point, I was not aware of how many foster homes I had lived in, I just wanted to see if I had any family still living. So I paid for a copy of my records, and took them home to read.

I spent the next few hours reading and re-reading some of the things that had happened to me. Apparently, I had lived in a total of 48 foster/group homes. Wow! I had no idea it had been that many! It boggled my mind. And then, I came across a list of relatives, their names, and phone numbers, one of which was my grandmother. So I called her. Of all people, the one who never believed anything I said. But she was family, and at that point she was all I had, or so I thought.

I went through the normal "Is this Margery Nichols?" routine. She seemed happy to hear from me, and I decided to see if maybe there was still a chance to have an actual, decent relationship with her. She then told me that my dad was living with her again, and that his wife (the one after Roseanne, aka The Stepmother) left him – I was SO HAPPY to hear that!

I spoke to my dad, who asked me to come and live with them in South Florida again.

After learning that my grandmother was still married to the man who had abused me as a child, I was hesitant, but my dad was there, and I was now an adult; there was no way this man would be dumb enough to try anything this time. Besides, by that point, I had learned how to stand up for myself. So, I agreed.

My dad paid for my ticket, I told my Pastor (Pastor A. L. O'Brien) the circumstances, and he gave me his blessing. I also told my landlady that I was leaving, and I would be back for the rest of my things. She said that she would put them in storage for me. I thanked her for taking such good care of me, and for making sure that I never did without a meal.

My landlady took me to the airport. I had never flown before, so this was going to be interesting.

I never did go back for my things. When I was finally in a place that I could go back and get them, I found out that her husband had already thrown them away. Their storage was an old apartment, and they needed to rent it out.

Brittany (left) & Chelsie

Chapter 4: Family and Marriage

WHEN I DISEMBARKED at Fort Lauderdale-Hollywood International Airport on October 26th 1986, and walked into the airport, the first person to greet me at the door was my daddy with a HUGE smile on his face. Standing next to him was my granny… and her husband.

I felt really weird and unsure know how to act. My daddy had rejected me, my step-grandfather sexually assaulted me, and my granny never believed me. But God helped me. We spent hours talking about what I had been through, and my granny kept saying that they had looked for me - I'm not sure how hard, honestly - but she and my daddy were there now, and that was what was important.

It didn't take long for me to find an Apostolic church in Fort Lauderdale, pastored by G. Oliver Barnes. So, that next Sunday, I had my granny drive me to his church. We sat in the parking lot for a few minutes, listening to the music, until I finally got up enough nerve to go inside. When I opened the door, I soon realized that I was the only white girl in that church.

This was nothing unusual for me, as my last year in high school I was the only white girl on the track team.

The service was powerful that day, and the Lord moved in a mighty way. Afterwards, Pastor Barnes came up to welcome me and tell me how glad he was that I came. I explained that I just moved back to the area and was looking for a church. He graciously told me that maybe I would feel more comfortable at another church, and gave me the number to United Pentecostal Church in Davie, pastored at the time by Reverend Gary Harris.

Pastor and Sister Harris were able to pick me up for church, since I lived not far from them. We had some great talks. Pastor and Sister Harris will always hold a special place in my heart.

During conversations with my granny, I found out that my grandfather, Sidney Levitt – granny's first husband – had left my brother and me an inheritance of a 1-acre lot in Ocala, and $250,000. Granny said that she divided that inheritance among her 8 children, but I think that she was the one spending it because one day I caught her grabbing something out of her drawer that had my name on it. When I asked her about it, she said she was using it for groceries. I had my family back, though, so I managed to push aside that additional betrayal, in favor of salvaging some sort of relationship with them again.

I was just starting to get adjusted to having a family again, when I met a guy in church. He played the guitar, and would travel around and preach where ever they would allow him. He seemed to be on fire for God, which is what drew my attention to him. But I dared not even look his way. I was really shy, and even to this day, I wait for the guy to make the first move. If he don't, then I don't!

One night, after a powerful service, he beckoned me over to him. Nerves and anticipation set my stomach in knots. Never before had a guy in church shown interest in me. We spoke for a little bit, and then he asked if I would have dinner with him sometime.

I wasn't sure about it, but heard myself say, "Yes."

Our first date was Thanksgiving. I had invited him to come over for dinner, and I cooked to impress. It went well, and we went out almost every night for the next few weeks. He asked me to marry him in December. I was scared, and so I said no; I wasn't ready. But he didn't give up. He asked me again a few weeks later, and this time I said yes.

We were married January 30th, 1987.

I STILL wasn't ready to get married, but he seemed so sure that we were right for each other, and I followed blindly.

We were married on the steps of the lake house at the back of the church property, at night. Neither of us had much money, so we scrambled to put things together the best that we could, and Sister Harris was a great help. We became caretakers of the church property, and lived in a small efficiency next to the lake house, with a small RV as our kitchen.

Soon after, Pastor Harris decided to build another, larger building at the west end of the property, as our new sanctuary. All of the church members pitched in. I was pregnant with Brittany, my firstborn, during this time, so I would take care of making sure that all of the workers had plenty to drink and eat.

Brittany & her husband, Noe

One Sunday, Pastor Harris said that we should all bring our old Bibles that were falling apart to the church. We were going to bury them in the foundation of the new sanctuary. So the next Saturday, we met at the new location with our old Bibles in-hand. Each member laid their Bible in the foundation framework, wherever we chose. Once that was done, cement was poured on top. That new sanctuary was built – literally – on the Rock!

Brittany was 3 days old when we had our first service in the new church sanctuary, and she was dedicated that very day. A prophecy was delivered over her, that she would be used as a vessel of praise for the Lord, and for many years now, she has used her voice to lift up the Name of the Lord in Praise!

Chelsie joined us a year and a half after Brittany, She was an unexpected miracle. Throughout my pregnancy with Chelsie, the doctors all told me that I was having a boy.

Imagine my surprise when she decided to announce herself!

I started to notice that my husband didn't come home until the wee hours of the morning. I would wait by the window for him on those nights, contemplating where he was.

Sometime during our five years of marriage, he became involved with another lady. She would call the house often. I became fed up to the point that one time, I picked up the phone, and said, "As long as he calls himself my husband, don't call my house again!"

She never called our house after that. He decided to leave on the day of our 5th anniversary.

I was 24, had two small children, and didn't know how to raise them on my own. I'd never really had a good example for a mother, so I didn't know what I was doing. But one thing I *did* know, was that my kids were *not* going to grow up without their mother!

I have never been so terrified. The unknown was a bottomless chasm at my feet. Sure, I had faced the unknown before, many times, but then I'd only had myself to fend for, and now, I had two precious, innocent souls depending on me. I had no idea how to help us, but I DID know the One Who could help. I spent many extra hours on my knees in prayer, those first few years after my marriage imploded.

I was shaken off-balance and numb, but I kept going to church, and God kept me through it all.

God knew who to place in my life. One of the ladies in the church and her daughter – Sister "Mema" Black, and Debbie – stepped up to help. They gave me a ride whenever I needed one, and were always there to help in other ways.

The girls and me, 1994

My husband was very verbally and physically abusive, which started about 7 months into the marriage, and add to that, my history of childhood abuse...I was just a complete mess! Pastor and Sister Harris were a huge help!

The girls and I were eventually kicked out of our apartment since I was not able to pay the rent on my own. He filed for divorce, giving me full custody of the kids, and he SAID that he would pay child support. I had no clue what was happening. What was child support? A divorce? He didn't allow me to work after we married, so when he left, I had no recent job experience. I didn't know what was going to happen to us, but I knew that I would be a constant, active presence in my girls' lives – no matter what!

I decided to go back to school. So I took a business class at Sheridan Vocational School just for a semester until I was able to get a job.

One day I got into the car that my husband had just purchased and was allowing me to use, and the gas tank was completely empty. I had the kids in the car to take them to Mema's house, so I decided to get out and lay my hands on that car and pray. God knew that I didn't have any money for gas, and no one to call for help. After I prayed, I got back in the car and turned the key, and the car started right up!

This was a faith builder for me that God was going to take care of us! After that, Pastor Harris gave me a little car so that we could get around.

Following our eviction, I was so ashamed. There was nowhere else for us to go, so I drove to the church. The girls and I slept in our car, in the parking lot, for two weeks. Pastor and Sister Harris lived on the other end of the property at the time, so I didn't think they knew about us sleeping in the parking lot. Pastor Harris did find out, and told me that we were to stay in the nursery inside the church, until they could fix up a room for us. Once again, I became the property caretaker in exchange for room and board. God was still with us!

The girls and Mema

After about a year living in the church, I was able to get myself together a little bit more with the help of Sister Harris, Mema and Debbie. While we were still living at the church, we had a kitchen, our own bathroom, so we were set.

We were still going through so much with my by-then backslidden ex-husband, that it took a huge toll on us all. But I was able, with help, to put myself through Massage Therapy School, and to continue to be a decent mother to my children.

I spent much of my days on my face in the sanctuary...a benefit of living at the church. One day, about a year after my divorce, when I was praying in the sanctuary, God showed me that my ex-husband would come up to me and apologize, sobbing and saying sorry for everything he had ever done to us.

This stopped my prayer dead in its tracks, and I laughed out loud at God!

My words were, "YEAH, RIGHT!"

I got up and didn't go back to pray for the rest of that day. My ex was so full of himself that the thought of him ever apologizing to ANYONE – let alone to ME – was truly laughable.

I forgot all about that promise, and moved on with my life with my children.

It was during this time that I decided to see if I could find my mother. I asked my dad for her birth date and the correct spelling of her name, and then I contacted the Davie

Police Department, and ask them to find her. I explained that I had lived in foster homes for most of my life, and just wanted to see if I could locate her, because I had so many questions.

About a week or so later, I received a letter in the mail from her, explaining that she was living in Palm Bay, Florida, just a few hours away, and inviting us (my girls and me) to spend the day with her.

The girls and I went to visit her, and she seemed so happy to see us. She made a coffee cup with our picture on it, and bought Easter dresses for the girls. We had a great time. During the visit, I asked why she left. She said, "If you only knew what your dad used to do to me."

I was so confused. I had never known my dad to be so violent, so I had my doubts.

We made plans with her to visit again on Mother's Day. I had FINALLY found my mom, and looked forward to having her in my life again!

We drove back up on Mother's Day, and I hoped to take her to lunch. But the family she had been staying with told me that *they* were taking her out for lunch. I was hurt, because the girls and I had driven 2 hours just to take my mom to lunch. But I agreed to go along with them, so as to not cause drama, and we went home.

A few days later, I received another letter from my mom, this one saying that she did not have room in her life for me.

WHAT?! Where did THAT come from?!

I decided right then and there that I had survived 21 years without her, and I could continue the rest of my life without her.

An unmarried gentleman came to service one night. I went up to him afterward with a word that I felt God gave to me for him. I told him not to leave that service until he received the Holy Ghost and was baptized in Jesus' Name.

He took that word to heart. I got a few of the men and women together, and by the mercies of God, we prayed Ed through to the Holy Ghost, and he was baptized in Jesus' Name that night!

Ed was attending Baylor University to become a podiatrist, and he made sure to call me every day. We became the best of friends; just friends. I helped him develop a prayer life, and he became a listening ear for me when I needed it. My children adored him.

Brother Ed will always hold a dear place in our hearts. We have kept in touch through the years. Last we spoke, he was living in Texas, and getting married to a lovely, godly lady.

I received news from my dad that my grandmother was very ill, and not doing well. She was moved to a hospital in Jacksonville, Florida, near one of her daughters. Since the girls were at their dad's house for the weekend, I made a trip to see her.

Unbeknownst to me, all of her brothers and sisters – my great-aunts and uncles – were there, most of whom I had never met.

After all of the greetings and introductions were said, we focused on granny, who was barely clinging to life. So I decided to get everyone gathered around the bed to sing. We did this every day.

One day she was more coherent than ever, and the nurse told us that this was the time to say our goodbyes. One by one we went in to say goodbye.

Just before I made the trip, I went to the state attorney to file charges against my step-grandfather since there was no statute of limitation on sexual assault at that time. However, when I got to the hospital, he was there.

Apparently, the state attorney had already contacted him, because as soon as he could get me alone, he begged me not to press charges.

"Dorothy, please, don't press charges against me. I'm so sorry for what I did to you all those years ago, but please. I don't want to go to jail!"

God was already checking me in the Holy Ghost about forgiveness, so I replied, "Okay. But I have a condition."

"Anything!"

"You MUST admit what you did to me, to granny, and in front of me. Right now."

He paled, and looked shaken, but after a few moments he said, "I'll do it."

We walked in to her room together, and approached her bed. "Granny," I said, "it's Dorothy. Can you hear me?"

"Yes."

I looked at him, and said, "Granny, your husband has something to tell you."

And he told her.

As the tears were running down her face, I felt forgiveness flow!

Was it easy? Absolutely not! This was not the last thing I wanted her to hear before she left this earth, but it was necessary for me to have some closure.

Aaliyah & Chelsie

Chelsie & Mema

Chapter 5: Building my Testimony

ONE DAY AFTER I RETURNED HOME from my granny's funeral, when Brittany was 4, and Chelsie was 2-1/2, my ex-husband picked them up for his regular weekend visitation. And then he called to say he wasn't bringing them back.

I was devastated! I didn't have his address, or phone number, since he refused to give them to me, and back then I didn't have caller ID, or a cell phone. I did not know what to do, so I hit my knees in prayer. I knew that God would help me.

The girls' father ended up keeping them for about 2 years.

A few months, later one of the men in the church came up to me and said, "Sister Dorothy, here is $500, go and get an attorney so you can get those girls back."

So I called around to find an attorney to take my case. Finally, I found one.

I began to build my case. I asked everyone I could think of – within and without the church – to sign a character witness letter, and filled up a whole page of signatures before the end of the day. I went to the attorney armed with those signatures.

I went to Brittany's school to show them that technically, I still had custody of her. This way I could be there for her in school to find how she was doing. Come to find out, her father changed her birthday on her school records to get her in school. So she actually started school at 4 years old.

The girls and me, 1996

By this time, my ex had started a few businesses, and was making pretty good money, but he always lied about it, claiming that he couldn't afford to pay child support. It wasn't just his word against mine, he also had the weight of a brother who worked at the Pentagon, and a cousin who was an attorney behind him.

BUT I HAD GOD ON MY SIDE!

It wasn't long before I had a home-study scheduled, so that I could petition the court to regain custody of the girls. At that time, he was threatening to take them permanently, and I just wasn't going to have it! If he wanted to fight for custody, a fight he would have!

Back then I was just in my late 20s and did not know the law. I was still naïve, and everything that he was doing – even though I knew it was wrong – I did not know what to do about it.

Their dad started building his own case … with false information.

On the day of my scheduled home-study, he brought the kids to me. Brittany, whose beautiful curly hair had been way down her back, was now cut all the way up to her ears, and her ears were pierced.

I was livid!

The home-study case worker was already there when he dropped them off, but I gave him a tongue-lashing. I didn't care if she heard me. I asked how he dared to do these things without speaking to me. He just laughed at me and left.

The case worker continued the home-study, and then left. A few weeks later, the results arrived in the mail. The case worker reported that I was an unfit mother because I was a religious fanatic! I went straight to the sanctuary and started dancing and shouting on the top of my lungs. That was the best compliment anyone could have given me!

I shared all of this with my friend Brother Ed, who was always such a great listener. He reminded me that God had it all under control.

I knew he was right, so I left it in God's capable hands, and waited for my court date.

My ex had remarried by this time, and because his wife's number was listed on the paperwork at the school, I decided to call. She answered the phone and we ended up talking about my home-study. She shared that my ex had used her money to pay off the lady who did MY home study.

I was stunned! I sent the court an email, detailing our conversation, and politely demanded an explanation. I never received a response.

A few days later, he came and dropped off the girls. Brittany, at 5 years old, had a bruise on her thigh, and not the kind of bruise a child of that age gets from regular play.

When I questioned her about it, she said that her daddy spanked her for something that she did wrong.

Now listen, I believe in spanking, but not if it's going to leave a bruise, and spankings belong on the sit-spot (aka, the behind), NOT on the thigh!

I called my pastor, and asked for his advice, because he knew my ex-husband as well. He told me to file a report, allow the police to take picture of the bruise and question the girls, but to not press charges.

I followed his advice to the letter, and left it in the Master's Hands.

A few days prior to the hearing, Debbie called and asked if I could pick her up from work. The girls were with their father that day, so I said I would.

As I was driving on I-95, an elderly lady right in front of me decided to stop in the middle of the road while everyone was going 65 or more miles an hour during 6 o'clock Rush Hour.

I slammed on my breaks and swerved to avoid hitting her, and lost control of my car. I spun across 5 lanes of traffic, and back again without hitting a single car, but I hit the median wall, spun across and back for a second time, again without hitting anyone, and hit the wall again.

When I finally came to a stop after the second time, I felt so weak, and everything was turning white. I remember praying, "God, please not now, my kids need me."

When I woke up, the firefighters were using the Jaws of Life to pry open my door. They asked if I wanted them to call anyone, and I requested that they call my pastor.

A helicopter had been requested to airlift me to the hospital, but since I woke up, the ambulance took me. I was still fading in and out of consciousness...my face and arm were bleeding...

After all was said and done, I only needed stitches in my nose and my elbow. There were no broken bones! I stayed in the hospital overnight for observation, and then I was released.

The devil thought he had me, but Jesus came and grabbed me! He kept me right in the palms of His hands!

The day of my hearing, I was still very sore, my face swollen, and black and blue from my accident. But these were my children, and I was going to fight for them, no matter what.

When I arrived to the Fort Lauderdale court house, my ex was there already, sitting in the hallway, waiting for the bailiff to bring us into the courtroom, and I sat down across from him. He was in full public-face mode, acting so sweet, telling me that he will allow me to see the kids whenever I want.

I just sat there thinking, *Man, you sure are sure of yourself, aren't ya?*

Then we were called into the courtroom.

The Judge flipped through the file, reviewing all of the paperwork, when she suddenly stopped, and looked at my ex with a VERY angry face! "How dare you hurt a 5-year-old like this!"

"But, Your Honor, I have a home-study case against her," he began, pointing at me, "and – "

She cut him off. "I don't care what you THINK you have. You will NEVER get custody of these children. As far as I'm concerned, you are the scum of the earth!"

We were in her courtroom for less than 5 minutes. I never had to speak a word; God spoke for me! From that point forward, he no longer tried to manipulate me! Was it smooth sailing after that? No, of course not, but God knew right where I was, and He was helping me.

On several occasions, Daddy would come to the church to visit me and the girls. Whatever happened between him and my mom, was left between him and her. I wanted my children to know their grandfather.

At one point, I also researched my mom's sister, Brenda. My mom had given me her phone number, so I gave her a call. We decided to go and eat pizza around the corner from her home in Hollywood. We spend hours talking and talking, My Uncle Frank apparently was a lobster fisherman. I'm not real sure if she told me where she worked but she seemed comfortable enough financially, so I wasn't worried.

A couple of years later, I met one of her sons, Roger. She told me another son worked for the Davie Police Department. I never did meet him.

After that visit, I didn't hear from her again until 2010, when she told me that my mom had passed in 2002, in Dothan, Alabama.

WOW! Really? Nobody thought to call me?

And so it continued. The questions just kept piling up.

Two years after that, Brother Harris stepped down as pastor of United Pentecostal Church in Davie, Florida, so I had to find another place to live. One of the other families in the church had a 3-bedroom house that was vacant, and offered it to us, rent-free, until I got back on my feet.

God had our back! I was faithful to pay my tithes when money did come my way, I never, ever missed a service, and I stayed prayed up, (I HAD TO!), so I accepted their generous offer.

God blessed us mightily!

This was when we learned the value of praying as a family and having devotions in our home. At 7:00 every night except church nights, the girls and I gathered in the living room for family prayer.

Because of what we had all been through, we had a lot of scars and issues still that we needed to lay at the feet of Jesus.

The girls and me, 1999

We heard of a little Pentecostal church called Calvary Life Tabernacle that met in a warehouse in Margate, and since we were currently without a pastor, we went to visit. This church was pastored by Reverend David and Sister Melanie Elms.

The girls loved it there, so we stayed. Brittany started on the Bible Quiz team under Danita Costas.

In 1997, the Board purchased the 5 acres of land and building of United Pentecostal Church in Davie that had been left without a pastor in the wake of Brother Harris' withdrawal, and the congregation of Calvary Life Tabernacle moved there.

Chapter 6: New Life Begins

I WAS ABLE TO FIND a 2-bedroom apartment within my budget, and life started to come together a little bit for us. We had a roof over our heads, which technically was my first apartment alone with the girls.

I was still not financially stable, working two and three jobs at a time to make ends meet. That the girls' dad still refused to pay child support didn't help any, and I just couldn't make it work for us financially. So we ended up moving in with a family in the church, Debbie and Von Hanner and their 2 boys, who were about my daughters' ages, with the agreement that I would pay them a certain amount of rent until it was time for us to move out.

I had just broken my ankle, so I was not able to work much. When my foot healed, I did get a job as a bus driver for Broward County Schools, which was helpful.

When we were able to move into our own place once again, Von and Debbie handed me back all of the money I had paid them for rent. Such a blessing I will never forget as long as I live! With that money, I was able to purchase a 3-bedroom mobile home. Within three months, the manager of the mobile home park asked me to step in as the park manager since she was fighting cancer and it was becoming too much for her to handle. I said yes.

One day on the way to church, driving from Pompano to Davie, (I had just purchased this old fix-me-upper car so that we could have transportation, and had a mechanic friend check it out to make sure that we wouldn't get stuck anywhere), I started to hear a little noise. I didn't say anything, just rolled down my window to listen, and then realized that the sound was coming from inside the car. I was looking everywhere, but couldn't figure it out, until I looked in the rearview mirror. And I watched and heard Brittany, at 9 years old, speaking in tongues! I got such a blessing watching and listening to her bless her God!

Brittany & Chelsie

Everything went well for a few years, and then I had a problem tenant who was friends with the district attorney, and so seemed to believe that he was entitled to do anything he wanted, and would get away with it. This guy refused to pay his rent, and when I served him eviction papers, he started his intimidation tactics. He would trap me in the office, and drive by my home real slow and glare at us in a threatening manner. One time, he even dumped horse manure inside my car when the sunroof was accidently left opened the night before. So, I decided to take my girls, and buy another mobile home in a nearby park.

Chelsie, Orange Blossom Festival Parade, 2006

We were only there long enough to fix it up real nice. We were just getting comfortable, and then unfortunately, Hurricane Wilma happened. The day before she hit South Florida, on October 24, 2005, we were told to evacuate the mobile home park. We moved into a townhome, and decided that if nothing happened to the mobile home, I would rent it out. However, Hurricane Wilma came through and demolished that mobile home.

Brittany, Orange Blossom Festival Parade, 2006

The girls began to excel in school to the point that they took advanced classes. They also participated in Bible quizzing. I was so proud of them! I grew ever stronger in my walk with God. We moved closer to the church, and were there every time the doors were open, even if we had to walk, which we did many times due to car trouble.

I still had not processed all of the years that I spent in foster care, much less a marriage, two children, and divorce within a 5-year period. I had a lot of growing up to do, and I had to do it fast for my children's sake. So we continued those family prayer meetings, and I kept them in Bible quizzing, because I knew that what I couldn't teach them, God's Word COULD!

Me, Orange Blossom Festival Parade, 2006

We learned so much at the Calvary Life Tabernacle, which was renamed Cathedral of Pentecost. I learned that it's not just about me, and my problems; there are actual souls out there who will go to a sinner's hell without God.

It's our mission to pour out what God has poured into us, and I witnessed to whomever would listen.

I brought a co-worker from American Express named Sherry to church, who received the Holy Ghost. I gave a Bible study to the maintenance guy's wife at the mobile home park that I managed at the time. She also received the Holy Ghost, and then brought her children, who also received the Holy Ghost.

God can use your situation to help someone else. He can change your mess into a message for His Glory! You may never know why you go through the things that you do, but know this, if you use your struggles to build your testimony, then not only will you win souls to God, but God will ultimately get all of the Glory.

Brittany, Church Work Day

Chapter 7: St. Cloud – More Scars, Then Healing!

AFTER 10 YEARS AT CATHEDRAL OF PENTECOST, I felt God call me to get out of my comfort zone. I heard about a little church in St. Cloud, Florida, that was really struggling. I wasn't sure how I could help, but I felt God pointing me in that direction. I brought it to Pastor Elms for his counsel, and he told me I should go. So, I uprooted my children from their friends and church to follow the will of the Lord!

I called the pastor of Souls Harvest Church to let him know that we were coming, with the blessing of our pastor. And without me even asking, he found a house for us to rent. That was such a blessing! I had a little money saved up for the move, but I needed to get a job right away, or we would not be staying there long.

We struggled that first year, and we moved a lot because of my inability to obtain a home that we could afford. Prices were not much better in St. Cloud than in Broward County. This caused bitterness in my youngest, who found solace with some kids she met at her new school. Her association with them was the final straw that caused her to backslide at 15.

I was broken again. I knew that I'd heard from God, so why was this happening? But I trusted God. And I held on.

I never really had to depend on my own income before to take care of my kids, I'd always had help, but now I was forced to make it happen. Trying to figure everything out on my own was stressful. I knew God could and would help me, but it seemed that He was trying to teach me to stand on my own two feet. We went from place to place, and I went from job to job. God made sure that we were never on the street, but it was really rough.

Me, at a Toastmasters of St. Cloud meeting, 2012

Pastor Shurte asked me to be the Ministry Secretary, and I was also a Sunday school teacher for the 2-4 year old children. It was one of my greatest joys, to be able to pour myself into these children. Sharing the love of God with them was such an honor and a privilege.

For the second time in my life, I was treated as a valued member of a church, instead of like a victim of my past! Pastor Shurte – like Pastor Elms – always made me feel needed, and my contribution, appreciated. Their confidence in me reminded me of the song "He saw not what I was, He saw what I could be." Pastor Shurte's confidence in me to be ministry secretary gave me the confidence that I needed to do the job!

Me and Brittany

This helped me to focus more on God, and not dwell so much on the tensions at home. This is where I learned the value of a prayer life, even more than during the drama with my ex. Now, it was literally becoming my lifeline!

There was one night that I was so mortified. Brittany had a friend come over to spend the night at the church, and Chelsie went to her new friend's house. It was getting late, I was texting Chelsie to come home, but no response.

At about 10 at night, the doorbell rang. This young teenaged boy had Chelsie in his arms, dragging along right beside him. This had never happened before! Her 14-year-old friend so calmly told me that she drank a whole bunch of liquor that night and she was plum plastered! I was in complete shock!

My daughter, who I raised in the church - I never drank in my entire life, she was never around such behavior at my house - was standing before me knocked out drunk! So after yelling at the top of my lungs - How could this happen? Who was the adult in charge? Who provided this stuff to my under-aged daughter? - I called the police and filed a report after I obtained that information. That guy, I was told, went to jail. But Chelsie already had a taste for it. So behind my back, she drank. I would never know, until she came home drunk.

I had finally had enough! I told her that if she could not follow my rules, she had to leave. It broke my heart to say such a thing, but tough love was required at this point. I always made sure that I knew where she was, and where she was staying without her knowing. I would ask some of her friends who would spill the beans.

She managed to graduate in spite of herself, and I did go to her graduation. But by this point, her new family had completely pulled my daughter out of the church. And I was supposed to be ok with that. But I wasn't; of course I wasn't. I prayed! I never stopped praying! Every time I went to the Lord about her, I got a vision of me carrying her laying limp in my arms before the Lord, (as if she just surrendered herself to the world)! But in my vision, when I would present her to the Lord, the Lord would pour His blood all over her. This would break me every time. She was my baby, she was in trouble, and I felt so very helpless! This other family continues to have influence in her life still today, 16 years later.

Brittany ended up going back to South Florida and attending the Pentecostals of Cooper City, pastored by Rev. Mark Hattabaugh. Since she was 17, she decided that she was old enough to move out as well. She didn't want to stay with her dad because she did not feel like his new (5th) wife accepted her at all, so she stayed with a family in the church until she could get her own place.

I was alone again, so I used this time to dive into working in and around Souls Harvest Church. I did whatever I could to help: teach Sunday school, sing, run media, ministry secretary…where ever I was needed, I helped to the best of my ability.

Brittany, high school graduation

I was not going to allow the devil to win the tug-of-war for mine or my children's souls! So many things I went through will never be published, but I will say this, I was so broken. I prayed for my children endlessly, but I felt like such a failure as a mother when it came to Chelsie. I could not figure out where I had messed up with her, but I laid her at the feet of Jesus, time and time again.

Me and Chelsie

Countless times when I was praying for my children, I felt God wrap His loving arms around me and say, "Dorothy, I've got them right in the palm of My Hand!"

One morning, after service, Pastor Shurte, (who knew everything) said to me, "Dorothy, this is not your fault. You raised them right."

This consoled me temporarily. I still had this voice of condemnation in the back of my mind saying, "You could have done more!" Although I'm not sure what more I could have done, I really did feel helpless.

One night when she was 16, Chelsie was at a friend's house drinking. She went up to the second story balcony, and decided it was okay to jump into the swimming pool. As a result, the retina in her left eye completely detached itself, and she went blind. She came back home for a while, and I immediately made arrangements to get her to Miami to this doctor who specialized in retina reattachment. After the surgery, there were some complications. Her eye pressure never went down, therefore the surgery did not take, and scar tissue developed all around the membranes of her eye.

She will never see out of that eye again unless God decides to heal her, which is absolutely possible!

A few years later, Chelsie started dating the leader of the Crip gang. I was devastated, but I knew that God was still in control, so I did not feel defeated. I did my best to be nice to him, but I warned him… if he ever did anything to hurt my little girl, he was going to deal with me! Of course, at that time I did not knew that he was a gangster… No matter, that gangster had nothing on my Jesus! I prayed for years that he would leave, or that they would break up.

And then one night, at 2 in the morning, I was awakened out of a deep sleep with a vision of Chelsie standing in the middle of the dance floor, her friends circled all around her. And in this vision, somehow I could tell that Chelsie had decided to come back to God, but just as that thought crossed my mind her friends started to tighten the circle, as if to prevent her from leaving. And then, as clear as I could hear my own voice, I heard God say, "She made her choice."

And I woke up screaming "NO!"

I immediately called Brittany, (yes, I woke her from her sleep), and said, "We have to pray NOW!" I told her what I saw, and we prayed and interceded for Chelsie's soul, like never before, expecting God to come through for us.

Chelsie, high school graduation

The next day, I sat Chelsie down, and told her about this vision in the middle of the night. I could tell that it rattled her, but not enough. She told her boyfriend about it, and he even came to church with her a couple of times. But I knew that if he didn't surrender, neither would Chelsie. He did not surrender, and so, life continued in this new "normal." I could not understand this. It felt as if my prayers weren't working at all. Something had to give.

I still had not really dealt with my past. I was too busy working, carrying my girls in prayer, and serving in ministry. Ministry became my life, and I loved every minute of it.

One year, Brittany called me to tell me that the townhouse that she was staying in was being sold, and she would have to move. I knew that Chelsie had her friends to lean on, and she would not do without. She really didn't want me around anyway, so, I spoke to Pastor Shurte, and told him what was going on. He told me to go, but expected me to come back when the situation was resolved. I agreed.

So I made the trip back to South Florida, and my church was able to help financially until we were able to find something affordable for Brittany, which we did eventually. I agreed to stay and help her with the rent until she could get on her feet. During this time, I witnessed how my daughter was able to sustain herself in the Lord. There were many days that she would spend in her walk-in closet with the prayer blanket that I crochet for her wrapped around her for hours on end. One day I timed her; she was in that closet for 8 hours, praying, and reading the Word, and seeking God for help. I was a proud mama! I couldn't fight this battle for her, but God heard her prayers, and she learned how to get her strength to fight…through prayer.

Eventually, I went back to St Cloud to be present for Chelsie. By that point, she was asking for my help, and when I arrived back in town, Chelsie met me and gave me the biggest hug. Prior to this, Chelsie had it in her head that she could not hug me anymore for some reason. She had pushed me away for so long, and I was in shock when she hugged me. Of course I hugged my baby girl right back. She was a very disrespectful little girl, who felt entitled to receive anything and everything, but that night, none of that mattered. She WANTED to hug me, and my heart melted and hurt for her, all at the same time. For many years she pushed me away and refused to allow me to speak into her life at all, almost to the point of refusing to admit that I was even her mother.

Three years later, Brittany came back home for a year or two. I was worried about her for a time, as well. The enemy was trying to steal both of my girls! But Brittany was able to keep going to church and pursuing her relationship with God, even through all of her struggles. She knew that if she would just surround herself with the people of God, she would be okay. She would call me almost every day, telling me of things she was going through, and I would pray with her over the phone. But I still felt helpless because she was so far away. When Brittany finally did get back in tune with God, and reconsecrated herself, she was able to help me to get Chelsie back in church.

I found a really nice home for us, a 3-bedroom and 2-bath house with a huge front and back yard that was built 8 years before we moved in. We had NEVER stayed in anything this nice before. It was just $1000 rent per month, so we all agreed to split the rent and make a go of it again!

Me, Brittany, Mema, and Noe

Brittany stayed for another year before she met a nice young man named Noe on a Christian dating site. He was an immigrant from Nicaragua, and had been living in Miami for about 9 years. After a while, he stole her heart, she moved back to South Florida, and they were married.

Chelsie, now an adult, stayed strong in church for 3 years. During this time, we built some new, better memories together. When she signed up for the Youth on Missions trip to Scotland and London with Pastor Hattabaughs' church, we made chocolate-covered strawberries, pretzel sticks, and other sweets to sell after church to raise funds. With passport in hand, and a praying mama, off she went! When she came back, something was different. I couldn't put my finger on it, but it was like she had decided that this Apostolic life wasn't for her.

Chelsie's graduation from Florida State University (FSU)

I asked her one day what happened on the trip, but she didn't want to talk about it. She hung on, though, and kept coming to church. But then she decided to allow a guy she went to high school with to move into our home. I protested, but she was an adult, and once again, I had lost control and influence over her. So, I prayed. Two years later, they broke up and he moved out, but Chelsie was still determined to do things her way.

She had a one-night stand that was life-changing: she was pregnant. She briefly reconciled with the guy who had been living with us, but it wasn't meant to be. He left again, this time for good. And I could only pray that she would rekindle her relationship with God, for eternity.

Chelsie & Aaliyah

Chapter 8: Aaliyah

AALIYAH DECIDED TO GRACE US with her presence on December 7th, 2019, at 4:21am. I was so blessed to have been in the delivery room to watch this miraculous experience! Also there to support and witness were Aaliyah's dad, Brittany, and two of Chelsie's closest friends.

Aaliyah

This time around, Chelsie and I were getting along much better, and it gladdened my heart. I refused to be a product of my past, and was determined to be there every step of the way for my grandchild, as I had been for her mother and auntie.

At 3 months old, Aaliyah developed COVID-19. At the time, she was the youngest child to have contracted it, so she and Chelsie were on the news a couple of times. Eventually though, she fully recovered, and life went back to our new normal.

I was still living in the house with Chelsie, and now Aaliyah, but I needed my own space, and they needed theirs, so I moved into a little efficiency that was financially perfect for me. I was able to pay my bills up through the end of the year, which was a blessing, since I was no longer able to work a typical job anymore.

I had developed some medical issues in my feet, and an old injury to my back had returned with a vengeance, causing radiculopathy, and neuropathy, as well as osteo-arthritis. My employer was generous enough to pay me long-term disability until I was approved for Disability through Social Security. During this time, I also started having issues with my knee, and needed surgery. Apparently on one of my falls, I tore my meniscus in 3 places. Now mind you, I was there for everyone. If they called, I was there, no matter what. But now with all of these health issues creeping up on me, my mind was playing tricks on me.

The enemy had a hay day. He started to tell me that I was not useful to anyone anymore. I was just a has been. Me! I did everything by myself, because God gave me the strength to do it. I never called anyone for help if I could do it myself. And now, I had no choice. But there wasn't anyone to call. Chelsie had a new baby and a full-time job, so she couldn't help, and Brittany was all the way in South Florida. No one was there for me. Despair set in. I could not be there for anyone else, and doing that made me feel closer to God because I was helping his people. And now, well I felt that had nothing left to give.

My dad and me

After the first year of Aalyiah's life, I got news that my dad, who had been living with a family friend for years, was not doing so well. He had developed the onset to dementia, so I decided to move back to South Florida to be near him. Of course, I went to my pastor to seek his counsel, and he gave me his blessing.

I was going to hate being so far away from Aaliyah, but I knew that only a 3-hour drive or 1-hour flight separated us, and I was once again living with Brittany, and her husband Noe.

Aalyiah and her Mimi

So that September, I made the move back to South Florida, and was welcomed back to Cathedral of Pentecost. It was so good to see that almost all of the people who were there when I left, were still there when I returned, and many more, besides. It was really hard at first, because it had been such an honor to serve Pastor and Sister Shurte for those 16 years. We had such a great connection, and I will always love their heart for God. I will miss them, but I needed to do this!

Even though my dad was not there for me through most of my formative years and in my youth, I felt like I needed to be here for him. But something happened when I moved back to South Florida, when I would call, my dad would not answer. So I would call the house phone. Again, no answer. Finally, after I left several concerned messages, the daughter of the family friend my father was living with called me, and told me that my dad doesn't have any money, and I was to leave him alone.

Imagine my shock at such an implication! So, did I move here for nothing? No! God has a plan.

That next Thanksgiving, Chelsie and Aaliyah came down to visit Brittany, her husband, and me, and we spent the day together as a family. I cooked the turkey and desserts as I always do, and the girls did the rest. We had an awesome time together, sharing the holiday with my family, especially since I never really experienced much family holiday togetherness growing up.

Christmas was a blessed time with all of the family as well. I found myself just sitting back and taking it all in. I read the Christmas Story (Luke 2), as I always do.

The entire holiday was magical – the gifts, the laughs, the picture-taking. Family! So *this* is what family feels like!

Debbie, holding Aaliyah, Mema, and Chelsie

Chapter 9: The Pathway to Promise

LOOKING BACK ON MY LIFE, I suffered more than my share of negativity. It would have been so easy to play the victim, because I *was* one. However, with hind sight, in each situation, I can see where God was walking with me through my storms. Once I knew that I could trust Him with everything, I realized that I now can be a VICTOR through Christ! I am now able to live in victory every day because I know who holds my tomorrow. As Romans 8:37 assures, we are more than conquerors through Him that loved (and loves) us!

You may ask, "Really?" Yes! With Him, we can live victorious every day. Am I always able to live in victory? NO! I fight my flesh just like you do! But when we know how to conquer that flesh, then we are victorious!

Do I wish that I'd had a normal childhood? Of course! I think that goes without saying. But I will tell you this, because of what I went through, I see things in ways that people who grew up with loving parents and a stable family life cannot. I have been able to connect to the hurting where others were unable. I have always said, (and honestly, I don't know who came up with this, but it's true nonetheless), "You can't have a message, without going through some mess." And "You certainly can't have a testimony without first going through the test."

Are you that one? Are you going through what seems to be an impossible situation? Do you feel like you can't hear God's Voice? Let me be the first to tell you, the teacher is always silent during the test. Hold on to what you know to be true! God's Word, and prayer! Get on your face before God, even if you can't speak, put on revival radio, or Holy Ghost radio, or some preaching from an Apostolic preacher, and just listen. Or you can even just play an audio version of the Bible. Get the Word in you, and just allow God to speak to you.

Brittany & Noe

We don't always have the ability to think correctly when we are in the middle of our troubles. This is why you get the Word in you, play it in song version, or audio, or even some Holy Ghost preaching. All of the above! And God WILL meet you there. I can promise you that! He did it, and still does it for me.

Once you are able to focus on God again, and renew yourself in the Holy Ghost, remember: God didn't fill you back up again so that you can keep it to yourself. Pay it forward! Find someone to pour into what God has just poured back into you. God went looking for that lost sheep. So many of us pray, (and trust me, I'm guilty) "God, please send someone my way who is hungry to hear about You." But, I believe that God gave us an example in the parable about the lost sheep. The shepherd went searching for that lost sheep, and didn't stop until he found it. That's what we should do – go search for those lost sheep, instead of waiting on God to bring them to you.

It's so easy to get into the mentality of me and mine when we are going through our troubles. If there is some way that you can just shake yourself, get out of your funk, and go searching for that one!

I know there are those who may say that you can't help others until you yourself are helped. I do believe this wholeheartedly, but don't get stuck – like I did – in the mindset that you are broken and can't help anyone. You'll get stuck, like I did every day, I begged God to fix me, until one day I realized how many people who need God that I

117

came into contact with on a daily basis, but because I felt broken and unworthy, I didn't stop to help them, and they kept walking. I can only pray that the mercies of God are with them, and for forgiveness for being so stinking selfish.

Did I intend to be selfish? NO! But all I could think about was me and mine, when there is a dying world out there, each one with a God-shaped hole in their life. If I can help just one, the Bible says in Luke 15: 7, "I say unto you, that likewise joy shall be in heaven over one sinner that repenteth, more than over ninety and nine just persons, which need no repentance".

The truth of the matter is, we will NEVER be good enough! We ALL fail every day, but the Bible says in Romans 8:1, "There is therefore now no condemnation to them which are in Christ Jesus." So stop allowing your mind to go there. There are souls that ONLY YOU will be able to reach. They need to hear YOUR story of deliverance.

I could not be here today writing these things to you, if I first did not go through and experience these things. You see, if it were not for God, I would fail in my own efforts. But with His strength and wisdom, I am able to move forward, and take as many as I can with me along the way. I am not at the top yet. NONE OF US ARE! Yes, we have mountaintop experiences, but you can rest assured that Satan will try his dead level best to make sure that we don't stay there long. So you may say what's the point if I'm just going to fail anyway? I'll tell you what the point is: it's only failure if you don't get back up and try again.

So GET UP!

The best way to get up is to fall on your knees before God and allow Him to help you back up. And once you are up, reach down for that one, and pull them up beside you. I truly believe that when you are climbing up the rough side of the mountain, find your footing, dig in, and reach for that one behind or below you!

Christmas 2021

I want to take a minute to mention this as well. The church is a hospital, you will not find any perfect people here, just a bunch of sinners who are forgiven! So a lot of times, your brothers and sisters who are sitting next to you in church could be going through the hardest battle in their life. If we are sensitive to the Holy Ghost, He will show us how to minister to them. They may have failed miserably, and are living in sin at home, but come to church to somehow try again. Instead of condemning them, restore them. The Bible says in Galatians 6:1 "Brethren, if a man be overtaken in a fault, ye which are spiritual, RESTORE such a one in the spirit of meekness; considering thyself, lest thou also be tempted".

Through all of my experiences thus far, I can truly say, thank You, Jesus! Because they have given me the tools to help someone else. Even though I never tasted alcohol in my life, nor did I have a desire to do drugs, I must ALWAYS remind myself that this was not because of my strength. God kept me, and He can keep you.

Jesus, I'll Never Forget

Oh, Jesus, I'll never forget
What You've done for me
Jesus, I'll never forget
How you set me free.

Jesus, I'll never forget
How You brought me out
Jesus I'll never forget,
No never.

Good-bye to Despair
by Dorothy Levitt

There once was a child without a home,
terrified and all alone,

desperately seeking for someone who cared,
carrying a burden that no child should bear.

Never could have been better off,
as far as food, clothes, and a bed so soft.

But inside was a broken heart,
because Mother decided to part.

On the other hand, Dad was home,
comforting himself in a soft tone.

But because Jesus was there,
I said good-bye to despair!

Acknowledgements

This book is dedicated first to God, for keeping me in the palms of His Hands!

And then to my children, Brittany R. Gadea, her husband Noe Gadea, Chelsie L. Enciso, and my grandbaby Aaliyah N. Lopez. I hope you will take these experiences that I have had and learn from them. You all are the driving force behind this book. I thank you all for your support in writing my testimony.

Thank you, Brittany and Noe, for believing in me, and pushing me to write this book. Thank you, Chelsie, for your photo expertise, and your support in writing this book. It means the world to me!

To all of my readers, this book is not intended to be a pity party for myself, nor to make me a victim in any way. Quite the contrary, it is meant to show that God can take a nobody, with lots of problems, and turn them into a child of God!

To Pastor Troy Shurte and First Lady Kimberly Shurte, I thank you for believing in me when I didn't believe in myself. Thank you for loving my girls and me, and for pushing me to become more like Christ.

To Pastor David T. Elms and First Lady Melanie Elms, I'm so thankful for y'all stepping in and steering us in the right direction when life seemed to overtake us. I'm so very thankful for the financial help when the girls were smaller;

without it, they would not have had a Christmas. Thank you for loving us.

So very thankful for Emery Press and its publisher, Wendy Garfinkle, who has helped me edit and publish this book. This would not be possible without your dedication and hard work.

Notes from the Author's Daughters

From Brittany: "Mommy, I love you with all my heart. You're the best mommy in the whole world, no matter what anyone says. Thank you for raising us in the church, so we could be saved, and for all the sacrifices you ever made for us.

Thank you for all the times you have woken up early, and lost sleep and comfort to pray and fight for us in the Spirit. And for all the times you prayed for what I wanted, even though maybe you knew it wasn't the best choice.

Thank you for all the times you sacrificed your health to fast for us, and for all the times you went hungry and were happy just to see us full.

Mommy, thank you for never giving up on God, and for being a Christian. Thank you for showing me what mommies are supposed to do. Thank you for loving my husband and for praying for him.

Mommy, I just love you and appreciate you so much, and I forgive you for anything YOU feel you may have fallen short of. I pray you can forgive me for not being a better daughter.

I love you. You are the best, and most beautiful mommy in the whole world. I still want to be just like you!"

From Chelsie: "Mom, remember all those times when we'd argue, and I would get really mad at you and say things I didn't really mean?

And remember when you told me NOT to do something and I did it anyway?

And remember those times when I was supposed to do something but didn't because I knew if I waited long enough, you would do it yourself?

Well, thanks for letting me live anyway!

Thank you for all that you do for me and Aaliyah. We love and appreciate you!"

About the Author

Dorothy has a passion for doing the work of the Lord, and has served in many capacities: as Sunday school teacher, in media and music, and as ministry secretary.

She is a Jack (Jill) of All Trades, but her favorite trade is being a mom to Brittany and Chelsie, and a Mimi (grandmother) to Aaliyah. She has been an accomplished massage therapist for 10 years. She has authored numerous poems, some of which have been published online. *From Bondage to Breakthrough* is her first book.

You can find Dorothy online at https://www.facebook.com/DorothyLevittEnciso.

Made in the USA
Middletown, DE
02 March 2023